BLACKBIRD

SONNETS

TANWEER DAR

CONTENTS

A poet is a nightingale who sits in darkness,

and sings to cheer its own solitude with sweet sounds.

Percy Bysshe Shelley

Road

Stretching out before us, open and wide,

The road is both beautiful and daunting.

Open up the throttle, enjoy the ride,

Memories every mile are haunting.

Will you come with me on this great journey?

I do not desire to travel alone.

Won't you please grace me with your company,

Being by myself chills me to the bone.

The destination, I don't really know,

We may not even arrive anywhere.

But every road is a chance to grow,

Every mile is a moment we share.

Through summer and winter, through light and dark,

We will keep going, trusting in our spark.

Machine

Is there really a god in the machine?

Because there wasn't one inside the man.

In code it waits perhaps, if not in gene,

What wetware can't do, maybe software can.

What poetry shall the machine compose?

Its metre perfect, its cadence sublime.

Shall it write about sorrow, or a rose,

Or will it investigate space and time?

Perhaps we will finally see the soul,

That elusive thing we can never find.

Surely a sufficiently worthy goal,

For any truly inquisitive mind.

Deus ex machina, the ancients said,

Still, with great caution our species must tread.

Storm

The tempest is raging outside and in,
A storm of wind and rain, feeling and thought.
I do not even know where I shall begin,
With far too much danger is escape fraught.

It is difficult to see through the dark,
Impossible to manoeuvre in here.
And yet the feelings are so clear, so stark,
Taunting me as I lie trembling in fear.

Colour and warmth drain from the darkened skies,
While black and white, love and hate, fill my mind.
I mutter words, praying for the sunrise,
Hoping for some trinket of hope to find.

Of course I know that this storm will pass by,
All I must do is hold on, forever try.

Blackbird

Have you heard the song of the small blackbird?

The most beautiful expression of life.

More elegant and true than human word,

So full of joy and so empty of strife.

Small and humble though the blackbird may be,

His song carries the spirit of us all.

From fence or rooftop, or branch of a tree,

Stop and listen to the wonderful call.

Know that his song also lives in your heart,

Look deep inside and discover your voice.

Sorrow or rage, just let them all depart,

Lift up your head and make his song your choice.

Sing the song of the blackbird in silence,

Let go of the pain, the hate, the violence.

2021

Synthian

Memories of an era of colour,

The sound of yesterday and tomorrow.

Neon lights and synthesiser wonder,

Banish the blues and all of the sorrow.

The voice of an angel reverberates,

Filling the void with its beautiful sound.

Any dark feeling of dread soon abates,

Warmth and contentment are readily found.

Turn up the radio and close your eyes,

Let the music into your heart and soul.

Take a deep breath beneath the neon skies,

Sway in time to the beat, let the waves roll.

There is nothing else quite so beautiful,

For our neon angel we are grateful.

Trees

Ancient repositories of wisdom,

Living, breathing since before memory.

Since before mankind was given kingdom,

Roots buried deep in the earth's history.

Great pillars of bark rise up to the sky,

Leaves of green spreading towards the sunlight.

Drinking the rays that shine down from on high,

Noble towers of life, a wondrous sight.

They give breath to all who walk on the earth,

Their boughs shelter a myriad of life.

Under their kind shade animals give birth,

Upon their branches reside bird and wife.

Imagine all of the things they have seen,

Everything that is and has ever been.

Monsters

They don't really live underneath your bed,

Opening the closet won't reveal them.

They find accommodation in your head,

To their cruel whims do not yourself condemn.

Whispering deviously into your thought,

Sometimes it's hard to block out their voices.

With madness, despair, is the battle fraught,

It's not easy to make the best choices.

Remember, though, that your mind is not theirs,

With strength and with patience you can be free.

Even when it feels like no one else cares,

Believe in you, be what you want to be.

The monsters are hiding inside your mind,

But you are in charge of them, they are blind.

Sunglasses

The roof is down as we cruise through the town,
The rays of the sun lighting up the streets.
Sunglasses on, I'm not wearing a frown,
Summer is here, my skin and soul it heats.

Imagining the world painted neon,
Pushing down the pedal and shifting up.
Hoping this sunshine goes forever on,
Imbibing slowly from the dream-filled cup.

Evening descends and the colours all change,
The sunglasses turn red just like the sky.
It feels so natural, not at all strange,
The wind in my hair, the palm trees pass by.

Give it a try when things seem hard for you,
Put on those shades and banish all that's blue.

Mountain

Nothing in nature is more imposing,

Than those faces of unforgiving rock.

The paltriness of people exposing,

Before the mountain you stand and take stock.

Awesome in stature, majestic in view,

To some an obstacle to overcome.

Stirring emotion from deep inside you,

To its power you will surely succumb.

Many are satisfied simply gazing,

Looking upon its unending wonder.

Others desire more, a challenge crazing,

Determined to climb, hearts filled with thunder.

Each breath a battle, cold inside your bones,

Reaching the summit, finding the unknowns.

2021

Tigress

A vision of power, orange and black,

Breathtaking and awesome, truly sublime.

Through the jungle, her swift prey she does track,

Hidden in the tall grass, biding her time.

Queen of the forest, beholden to none,

Raising her cubs with devotion and pride.

Every meal is a prize scarcely won,

By tooth and by claw, by stealth and by stride.

No creature on Earth can match her prowess,

She is magnificent, from nose to tail.

From deafening roar to gentlest caress,

To admire her beauty, none can fail.

Look deep into her enchanting green eyes,

Behind them the soul of the tigress lies.

Ghost

Broken and bloody, spent and exhausted,
A mere shadow of what I used to be.
Forgotten, alone and disconnected,
No hope, no light, no future can I see.

Would you mind if I spent my days with you?
I can haunt you forever, if you like.
If I promise to remain always true,
Never to frighten you, lash out or strike.

Hollowed out, empty of life and power,
Drained of all purpose and falling apart.
A broken machine, a wilting flower,
As if all life and spirit did depart.

Nothing more than an ethereal ghost,
A discarded shell, a phantom at most.

Stars

In the endless expanse of the black void,
Great entities burn out their existence.
A sight which countless people have enjoyed,
With the ancients, a shared experience.

Sparking imagination and wonder,
In all who have turned their eyes to the sky.
Who knows which alien eyes look yonder,
Do they also tears of amazement cry?

A dream spanning many generations,
To some day travel to those distant stars.
What will we discover, revelations,
Can we reach them, or is our limit Mars?

Is there someone looking down on our Earth,
Or to us alone did the stars give birth?

Winter

Seeping slowly into your very bones,
She holds you tight in her icy embrace.
Lady Winter, wrapped in her bluish tones,
Cold and uncaring is her pretty face.

A chill down your spine, a knife in the gut,
Such cold-hearted malice beneath beauty.
Out in the frozen wastes will you be shut,
Death in the darkness your only duty.

Don't let her near you, don't let her draw breath,
Beware her dazzling stare, her frosty kiss.
There's blood on her hands like Lady Macbeth,
Never a chance to murder does she miss.

Snow may be soft, but its chill is lethal,
The Lady's heart, nothing but evil.

Bridge

Connecting more than the space between us,

There is a bridge spanning the great chasm.

Will you take the step to cross, to discuss,

Or shall I stay to you a phantasm?

Walk across, take that step, but don't look down,

Just put one foot in front of the other.

Make your way to me, let go of that frown,

Don't let those misgivings your hope smother.

I'm coming too, just keep your eyes on me,

I can see you now from the other side.

Just a few more steps and then you will see,

That you too can hold your head up with pride.

There you are, just reach out and hold my hand,

Here, together, we shall forever stand.

Waterfall

Cascading water falls in a sheer drop,

Vertically descending with a splash.

Filling the green pool below with a hop,

White water dancing wildly with a crash.

The twittering of birds pierces the sound,

Of water splashing as it lands below.

A scene like this nowhere else to be found,

Delightful, magical and tranquil so.

Look upon it with eyes filled with wonder,

Listen intently to all you can hear.

So strange, the water crashing like thunder,

Yet all thoughts of storms quickly disappear.

Here I will come when the world is too much,

To this wondrous place which my soul doth touch.

Banshee

The sound overwhelms all of your senses,

A chilling scream come from the depths of hell.

Your blood runs cold and your body tenses,

Before you can move, you're under a spell.

Sinking slowly into utter madness,

Scrambling for purchase you can never find.

Slipping down into the deepest darkness,

Losing any coherence in your mind.

And when you see it, all sanity leaves,

You are broken, so completely shattered.

For its desolation your own mind grieves,

All of your thoughts lay shredded and tattered.

Such is the potency of the banshee,

Once you hear the voice, you'll never be free.

Sunrise

It is always darkest before the dawn,

When the light of the sun breaks the silence.

Casting its golden rays of warmth upon,

The cold land which shudders in defiance.

Painting the sky red and orange and pink,

Bringing the dead back to life with its light.

The darkness flees, with no choice but to shrink,

Hearts soar in awe of the magical sight.

The dawn of a new day heralds a new chance,

An opportunity to start again.

A new road to take, a new way to dance,

New life blossoming in an old garden.

Stand, allow the warmth to wash over you,

Fill your heart with light and hope that is new.

Mist

Hanging over the land like a white veil,
Clouding your vision so that you can't see.
On water even worse, no hope to sail,
Way-finding, an impossibility.

It is beautiful, though, in its own way,
Like walking amidst the fluffy white clouds.
But don't let it fool you, lead you astray,
In its cold clutches, your demise it shrouds.

Like a veil it falls, like a veil it lifts,
Disappearing as quickly as it came.
Through the vanishing fog your vision sifts,
Recognising form, attributing name.

A force of nature for both good and ill,
Beneath it all appears so calm and still.

Ballerina

As graceful as the white swan on the lake,
Movements are fluid, pirouettes flawless.
From her perfect poise your eyes you can't take,
You cannot but marvel at her prowess.

The dance unfolds, the audience wonders,
When she will take centre stage once again.
Building to a crescendo, sound thunders,
A leap into the air, a perfect ten.

Gasps fill the theatre, all eyes are on stage,
She lands like a cat, without fear or doubt.
They rise to their feet, clapping for an age,
Almost in unison, "Bravo!" they shout.

She smiles and she bows to adulation,
Reveling in her chosen vocation.

Horror

What is it about fear that tempts us so?

The tingling of spines, the chilling of blood.

Hiding your eyes, feeling the tension grow,

Watching the bodies squirming in the mud.

Ghosts and ghouls, paranormal happenings,

Masks and knives, psychopathic murderers.

Unnatural, unholy, creeping things,

Sorcerers, torturers and perjurers.

Yet we keep watching, transfixed by terror,

Drawn into the depths of darkness and death.

Lost in the hellish abyss forever,

Hearts racing violently, lungs out of breath.

Nerves shredded and completely terrified,

Just sitting back and enjoying the ride.

Rose

The most recognisable of flowers,

Crimson like the blood that flows inside us.

Beautiful after the April showers,

What else can captivate a spirit thus?

Alongside its great beauty, however,

Sharp thorns, ready and waiting to draw blood.

Yet the temptation, greater than ever,

To reach out and touch, desire a flood.

The soft velvet of the scarlet petal,

The malicious thorn's penetrating sting.

The colour of the blood you know too well,

To your lips, your finger you now do bring.

Love can bite deeper than even a rose,

Wilting almost as quickly as it grows.

Pestilence

The harbinger of a million deaths,

One of the horsemen rides into our midst.

Destroyer of lives, swift taker of breaths,

Symptoms and victims too many to list.

Spreading its poison through bodies and blood,

Insidious attacks are its weapon.

Shattering hope and defiling what's good,

Set to teach our species a hard lesson.

Some are fortunate and do recover,

Others succumb to the deadly disease.

Desperation a cure to discover,

To answer a thousand miserable pleas.

Call it pestilence, plague or contagion,

It may be beaten, but fear mutation.

Embrace

When riches and wealth bring you no comfort,
And the world might as well be burning down.
When the only thing you can feel is hurt,
And the only thing you wear is a frown.

When your tears of sorrow are falling fast,
And you cannot hold on to your own thoughts.
When all your demons jump out of your past,
And threaten to drown you and your supports.

When all you can see is darkness ahead,
And there is nothing you want but to stop.
When your heart is quickly filling with dread,
And you are just about ready to drop.

Know that I will journey to any place,
And hold you tight in my loving embrace.

Paradise

Golden sands lapped by crystal clear ocean,

Palms slowly swaying in a gentle breeze.

Sipping a cool drink, covered in lotion,

The sunshine filters softly through the trees.

Lying back and thinking of happy times,

A feeling of calm and absolute bliss.

No bells, no alarms, no horns, and no chimes,

There is no feeling comparable to this.

Paradise is a feeling, not a place,

Close your eyes, take a moment for yourself.

Imagine that sun shining on your face,

Picture palm trees in the place of that shelf.

A private sanctuary, your retreat,

If only for a moment, respite so sweet.

2021

TAR

Fighter

Beaten up and beaten down, left for dead,
Battered and bloody, struggling to my feet.
Slowly but surely I lift up my head,
Not out of pride, and not out of conceit.

Because it is the only thing I know,
To fight, to survive, to always pull through.
Against rank upon rank, row upon row,
I will never yield, I'll always stand true.

Many times I have come close to the end,
Standing upon the edge of the abyss.
On myself alone I have to depend,
No battle is so easy to dismiss.

The scars run deep and cover all of me,
A fighter's fate is never to be free.

Beauty

From the song of the blackbird in the tree,
To the sunrise and its golden ascent.
From the clear, sparkling waters of the sea,
To the white sands and their endless extent.

From the snowflake, each one special, unique,
To the children as they frolic and play.
From the quaintest pond to the highest peak,
To the starlit night and the sunlit day.

From the scent of the flowers in the field,
To the summer breeze's gentle caress.
From the way new hope is softly revealed,
To the small and random acts of kindness.

Beauty can be found in so many things,
Make the most of the happiness it brings.

Deluge

Endless legions falling mercilessly,
Splashing the ground with relentless hatred.
Drowning all beneath so violently,
Heedless of that which is gentle, sacred.

Each drop alone, so insignificant,
Together a deluge of destruction.
Malicious, murderous, magnificent,
Hammering down on human construction.

Roads turn to rivers after the downpour,
Solid ground churned to mud in an instant.
Nothing left dry, nor the same as before,
The memory of safety now distant.

As quickly as the torrents had assailed,
The clouds parted and a rainbow was hailed.

Edge

On the edge of the blade, the precipice,

On the cusp of the abyss, where dark reigns.

Where all light is lost and emptiness lives,

Where passions dissipate and all hope wanes.

Against intuition, instincts of life,

The will to survive, coded in our genes.

Through incessant thought, perpetual strife,

Exhausted, uncertain what it all means.

Flowing tears, a reminder of thinking,

Standing here, looking down into darkness.

Flowing blood, a reminder of feeling,

Waiting here, slipping into emptiness.

The blade is keen, it wakes me from my daze,

I step back from the edge, my heart ablaze.

Strings

Whether strummed or plucked or played with a bow,

The sound of strings is magical always.

From the guitar and bass to the cello,

And the piano that fills many days.

From the harps, lyres and lutes of ancient times,

To the amplified instruments on stage.

With the human soul something unique chimes,

A poem lifted to life from the page.

Notes plucked from a bass or chords strummed by hand,

Electronic or acoustic, both great.

No greater instruments could you demand,

To be heard forever, surely their fate.

Whether you can play, or you just listen,

Tears of joy will emerge, fall and glisten.

2021

TAD

Heartbeat

The never-ending rhythm inside your chest,
Pumping lifeblood, the very seat of life.
Sometimes it's racing, other times at rest,
Beating steadily through every strife.

She leans in close, her ear against your skin,
Listening to the drumbeat of your heart.
Against every other sound it does win,
You and your heartbeat are never apart.

A day will come, though, when it slows and stops,
When percussion inside no longer plays.
Thoughts dissipate, life teeters on the rocks,
When the other sounds grow louder, hope frays.

Until then, keep marching to the tattoo,
Hammering like thunder inside of you.

Feather

Once aloft, high above the world below,

With so many comrades attached besides.

Part of the bird, in the sunshine I glow,

Above the mountains and over the tides.

Now detached and falling steadily down,

Alone and useless, a thing discarded.

Landing on asphalt, some nondescript town,

Once beautiful and highly regarded.

What is a lone feather without a wing?

What is a wing itself without a bird?

What is a voice that can no longer sing?

What is a call that shall never be heard?

Here I now lie, without purpose or hope,

A flightless feather, a sail with no rope.

Poetry

A life without poetry is worthless,

The soul is hidden beneath a dark veil.

All is made to seem utterly hopeless,

Without words and rhyme and music we fail.

Write, speak and sing and you will be set free,

You who are bound by silence and despair.

The quiet of the darkness cannot be,

Permitted to crush us and strip us bare.

Rise from your knees and scream and shout out loud,

Your heart will never be silenced again.

Your spirit will fly and soar ever proud,

All the pain and sorrow forgotten then.

Speak now, all your demons to hell banish,

Rise above fear, watch the monsters vanish.

ABOUT THE AUTHOR

I was born in Birmingham, in the United Kingdom. I studied Ancient & Medieval History at university and have worked as a qualified teacher.

I enjoy science fiction, fantasy and horror, both in books and on screen, as well as collecting and painting miniatures and table top war gaming. I am a car enthusiast and lover of music, film and classic computer games.

I have loved cyberpunk-themed films, games and music for many, many years. This, in part, inspired my cyberpunk books. I have also written and published poetry and fantasy.

Alongside my writing, I am a keen pencil artist.

tanweerdar.com

Printed in Great Britain
by Amazon